SANTA CLAUS
SNOWMAN

CHRISTMAS STOCKING
ELF
GIFTS

REINDEER
GINGERBREAD

CHRISTMAS TREE

ELF

CUT AND PASTE

Your opinion is very important for me.
If you can take a moment to leave me some feedback,
I would greatly appreciate it.
Thank you!

polifonia.kdp@gmail.com

see also part 1 and part 2

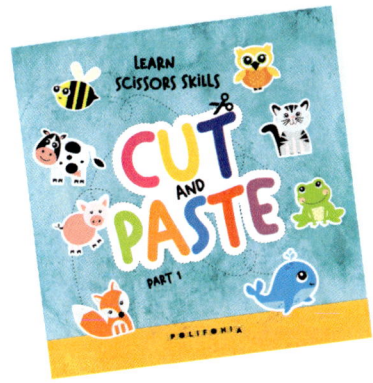
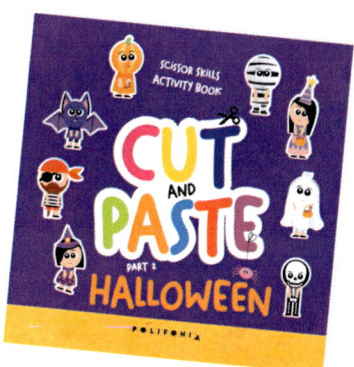

activity book by EVA LUSZCZ / illustrations by AGA ODRAKIEWICZ

Made in the USA
Las Vegas, NV
06 November 2022